# It's Good For A Girl To Know Who She Is

A fun and exciting tween workbook exploring
YOUston and the best parts of you

By Karen Howard

A workbook for girls 8+

iGrowGirl
encouraging girls to know who they are
and be the best they can be

ISBN 0692834338
ISBN-13 978-0692834336

Printed in The United States of America

This book is the first in a series of iGrow Girl workbooks. Our goal is to encourage girls to know who they are and be the best they can be.

The iGrow Girl learns about her likes, dislikes, personality traits, and strengths. She finds positive ideas and habits that will help her improve herself and inspire others. She is happy to learn new ways to make good choices. She works to do her best and to grow in her studies, her relationships, and her health.

An iGrow Girl also learns about words and habits that are not positive. When those words describe her behavior, she stops what she's doing and chooses to think and behave in a better way. By the time you finish this book, maybe you will become an iGrow Girl!

# Table of Contents

**Introduction...5**
Note to the Girl Reader...5
Note to Mom, Guardian or Mentor...6
Meet the Girl Guides...7
Map of "YOU"ston...8

**Part 1 - The Outside of You...9**
Mirror Lake...10
Point of View Trail...16
Closet Cave...21
Brain Snack Shack...25
Gateway Pass-Word...27

**Part 2 - Checking The Inside Out...28**
"A Mazing Personality"...29
Inner Me Market...36
Family Tree...40
Friend Observatory...45
Fun Center..48
School House Rock...51
End of Tour Pass-Word...55

Certificate of Completion...58

# Introduction

To the Girl Reader:

This book is about **YOU**! It's a fun tour of YOUston, an adventure where you will learn and explore the parts of you that make you who you are. While you are learning about yourself, you may come across a word or an idea that you don't completely understand. If that happens, look up definitions in the dictionary or other kid friendly internet sources, or ask a parent or trusted adult for help.

## It would be fun to complete the book any of four ways...

1. On your own.
2. With your mom or an older trusted female friend or relative.
3. With a group of friends.
4. With your mom and a group of friends with their moms.

Either way, this can be a great adventure! So choose the way that works best for you.

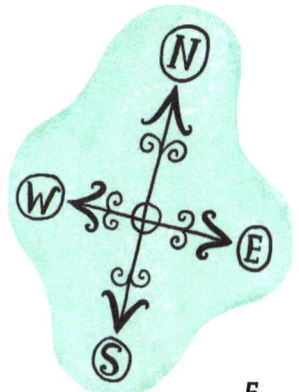

## To Mom, Guardian or Mentor:

This is a wonderful opportunity to learn more about your girl. Whether she decides to complete the book along with you or share her answers with you after she completes it on her own, each page will present opportunities to have meaningful conversations on a long list of topics - some of which you may not have even known were important to her.

You will never regret investing the time to strengthen the special bond between you and your girl by taking this fun journey of discovery with her. It's a great way to remind her that you are her biggest cheerleader and build a lasting foundation of open communication.

Melissa

Myah

Iko

# Meet the Girl Guides

The Girl Guides, Melissa, Myah, and Iko will lead you on the tour of YOUston, and they are anxious to get started.

Have you noticed anything special about the girls' names?
The first two letters of Melissa's name spells "me."
The first two letters of Myah's name spells "my," and the first letter of Iko's name spells "I."
That's "me, my, and I"— and they are here for YOU!
The iGrow Girl motto is "I grow. You grow. We grow together."

# Map of YOUston

The map below displays some important parts of YOUston that the Girl Guides will help you explore:

The first part of this trip will focus on your outward appearance and your point of view or your opinion on outward beauty. Later on, you'll think about inner beauty as you take a look at the people and places that are important to you,  and explore your own personality.

The following pages include questions that will help you organize your thoughts and keep a record of your discoveries.  Be honest with your answers! You are unique, and there is no one else exactly like you. No one can be you as well as you can. And you can't be anyone else better than you can be yourself.

You may think you already know all there is to know about yourself, but it's possible that you will be surprised by some of your answers!

# Part 1
# The Outside of You

# Mirror Lake

## See yourself

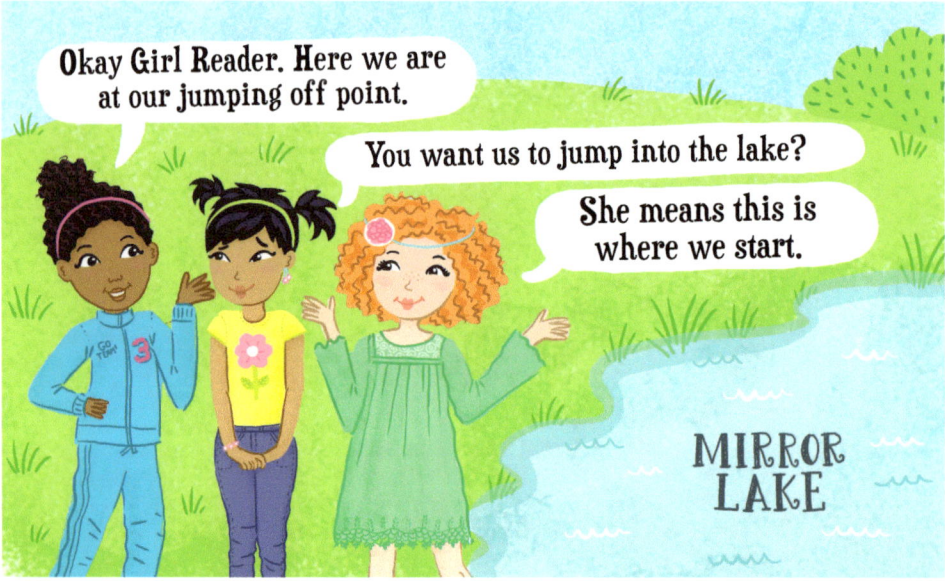

**Okay Girl Reader. Here we are at our jumping off point.**

**You want us to jump into the lake?**

**She means this is where we start.**

MIRROR LAKE

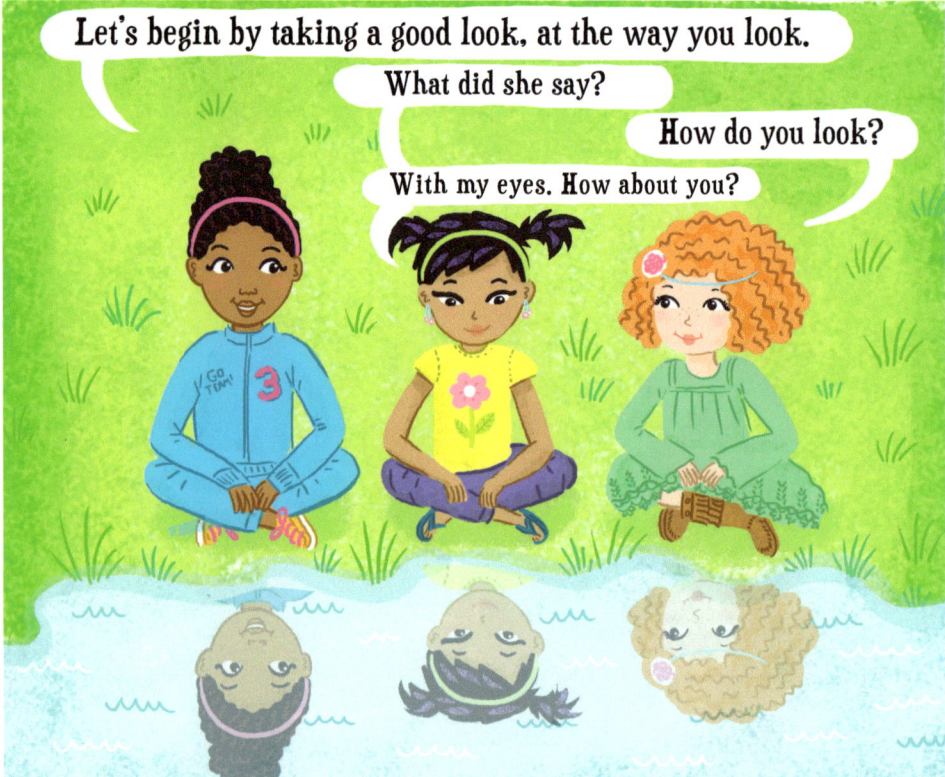

**Let's begin by taking a good look, at the way you look.**

**What did she say?**

**How do you look?**

**With my eyes. How about you?**

Find a full-length mirror and stand in front of it for a couple of minutes. Carefully examine your body from head to toe. Use the descriptions below to describe how you see yourself.

## Circle the word that best describes your...

### Height
Very Tall
Tall
Average
Short
Very Short

### Clothing Size
Small
Medium
Large

### Hair Density
Very Thick
Thick
Average
Thin
Very Thin

### Hair Texture
Straight
Curly
Coarse
Kinky
Wavy

### Natural Hair Color
Black
Red
Dark Brown
Light Brown
Blonde

### Hair Length
Really Short
Short
Shoulder-Length
Long
Really Long

# Circle the shape that's closest to the shape of your eyes.

## My eyes are shaped like...

Almonds

Grapes

Blueberries

Lemons

# Circle the shape that's closest to the shape of your face.

## My face shape is...

Round

Oval

Square

Oblong

# Write a phrase that describes your skin tone.
# Use these examples to get your creative juices flowing.

_____

_____

_____

_____

_____

_____

_____

Dark Chocolate

Honey Butter

Mocha

Peach

Vanilla Cream

Caramel

Choose a crayon or marker that is similar to your skin color. Use it to circle the picture of the nose that is most like yours or you can draw your own nose.

Choose a different crayon or marker. Use it to circle the lips that are most like yours or you can draw your own lips.

List two things that you like about the way you look.

1. _____

2. _____

If you're completing the book with someone, ask her to write two things that she likes about the way you look.

1. _____

2. _____

It's great that each of us is "one of a kind" —on the outside as well as the inside. Write one thing about your outward appearance that makes you unique.

1. _____

Is there anything about your outward appearance that you wish you could change? If so, what would you change and why?

_____

_____

If there is something about your outward appearance that you are not happy with, talk to your parent or a trusted adult about the way you feel. There are also a few suggestions outlined later in Part 1 — Brain Snack Shack that should help you to remember how special and beautiful you are!

# Use these clues to solve the puzzle.

1. The silent letter in the name of a small fragment of bread.
   *Hint: The word rhymes with plum.*

   _____

2. What is a female sheep called?
   *Hint: The word rhymes with two.*

   _____ _____ _____

3. A beverage which can be served hot or cold.
   *Hint: The word rhymes with sea.*

   _____ _____ _____

4. The opposite of empty.
   *Hint: The word rhymes with bull.*

   _____ _____ _____ _____

## Make one word from these four: _____

Answers: b-ewe-tea-full   beautiful

## Does this word describe your outward appearance?

_____

## Does this word describe every girl's outward appearance?

_____

Every girl is beautiful, including you!
And if you look for beauty in yourself
and others, you will find it.

# Point of View Trail

## See the outside of other girls

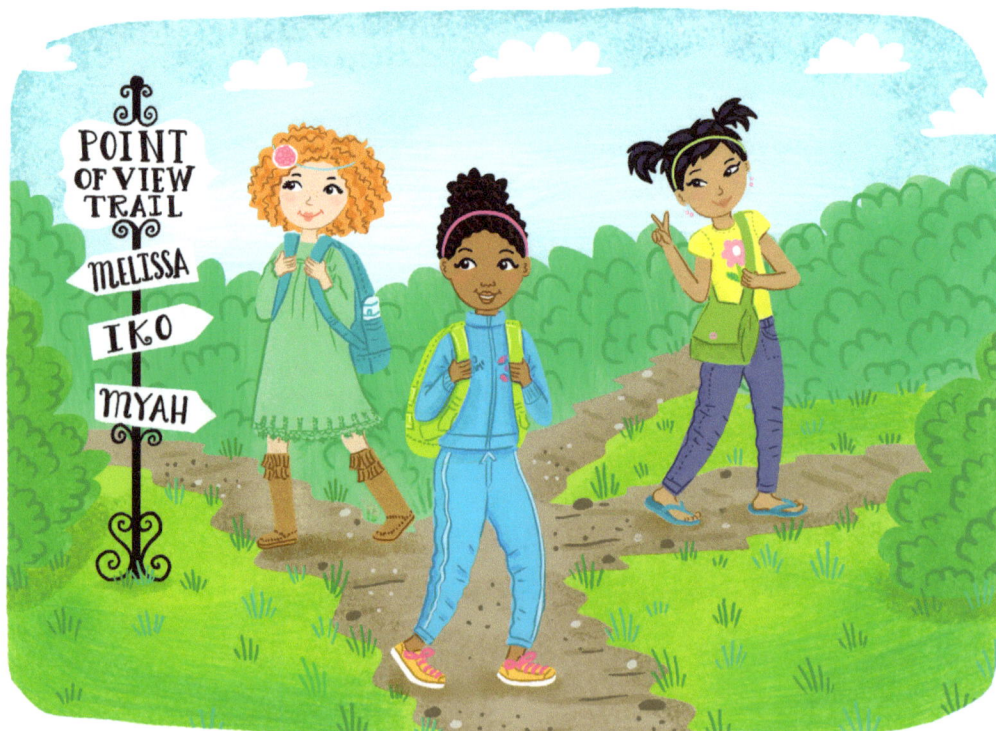

Here is where you take a hike with the Girl Guides. Each of the girls has chosen a different path or different point of view. As you get older you will need to think and talk about your point of view or opinions regarding many subjects. The following questions will help you discover more about your opinions on outer beauty.

This girl is from the Matses tribe in the Amazon Rainforest. Some girls of the Matses tribe wear facial tattoos and whiskers made from the veins of palm leaves. Can you see her beauty?

What makes her beautiful?

_____

_____

This girl is from the Maasai tribe of Kenya. Many Maasai girls wear brightly colored clothing and beads and often shave their heads.

What makes her beautiful?

_____

_____

17

This girl is from the Paduang or Kayan tribe of Thailand. Some Kayan girls wear neck rings made of brass to lengthen their necks.

## What makes her beautiful?

Learning about girls from other cultures and their ideas of what is beautiful is a good reminder that the world is a big place and is full of many different points of view on outer beauty.

Since opinions about beauty vary from one culture to another, and are likely to be different even among girls in the same culture you might wonder, "Who decides what real outer beauty is?" The answer is everyone and no one. Everyone has their own idea of what is beautiful, but no one should insist that every girl follow their "beauty" guidelines. It can be confusing, but try to remember to look for beauty in yourself and others. It would be useful to remember the tips below:

1. Every girl gets to have her own opinion, and one girl's opinion is just as important as any other.

2. It's great when we listen to others and share our opinions with kindness and respect - even if we don't agree.

**3.** It's not so great when we hurt others and make them feel badly because they see things differently.

**4.** Keep in mind that sometimes it's impolite to share your opinion when no one has asked for it. If sharing your opinion is going to be hurtful to the other person, it might be better to keep your opinion to yourself.

Macie is the new girl in your class. Her hair is kind of frizzy and she always pulls it back in a bun. Some of your friends have not learned to see beauty in every girl, and they make mean comments to you about Macie's hair. Based on what you've learned, what will you say to your friends?

_____

_____

_____

# Closet Cave

## Choose your style

**Closet Cave is all about your taste in fashion.
Answer these questions to reveal the look you like.**

1. It really doesn't matter what I wear. I'm not that interested in fashion.

   T    F

2. Keeping up with the latest fashion is very important to me. I think about it all the time.

   T    F

3. I care about what I wear, but I don't spend a lot of time thinking about it.

   T    F

4. If I like an outfit, I'll wear it. It doesn't matter what other people think.

   T    F

5. I take care of my clothes by hanging them and folding them neatly.

   T    F

6. I would rather be late for a party and look fabulous than to be on time and just look okay.

   T    F

7. Sometimes, what you wear can say a lot about your values and personality.

T    F

8. I love to wear jewelry.

T    F

9. Rate the following in the order of most favorite (4) to least favorite (1).

_____ earrings

_____ necklaces

_____ bracelets

_____ rings

10. I think body piercings are cool.

T    F

11. If allowed, I would pierce my (check all that apply):

_____ ears

_____ ears-multiple times

_____ nose

_____ eyebrow

12. I think tattoos are really cool.

T    F

13. When I'm older, I would like to have _____ tattoo(s).

_____ no

_____ one

_____ several

_____ a lot of

14. A girl should find one hairstyle that works and stick with it.

T    F

15. It's good to try new hairstyles regularly!

T    F

16. My hair has to look good, so I spend a lot of time on it.

T    F

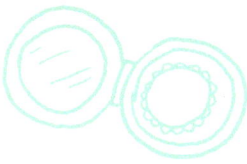

**17.** I spend

_____ no

_____ some

_____ lots of

time on skin care.

**18.** I try to keep my hands and feet looking nice and feeling soft.

T     F

**19.** Getting a zit is no big deal. It will eventually go away.

T     F

**20.** At the first sign of a zit, I do my best to hide it or get rid of it quickly.

T     F

**21.** A girl should be allowed to wear make-up when she's _____ years old.

**22.** A girl should

_____ always

_____ never

_____ occasionally

wear make-up.

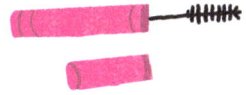

**23.** It's best to wear

_____ no

_____ a little

_____ a lot of

make-up.

**24.** I would like it if someone told me that I look older than I really am.

T     F

**25.** When I wear nail polish, I choose (Check one or more.)

_____ dark

_____ soft

_____ bright colors.

**26.** I don't care if the polish on my nails is chipped and worn off.

T     F

23

*Describe your style. (Example: girly, quirky, sporty, etc.)*

------------------------------------

------------------------------------

------------------------------------

**What do you like most about your style?**

_____

_____

_____

_____

*How do you think your friends and family would describe your style?*

_____

_____

*How do you think your style will change as you get older?*

_____

_____

_____

_____

Hopefully you've had fun taking a close look at your outward appearance and your sense of style. It might be easy to change your style and taste in fashion if you see new things that you like better. But there are things about your body or physical appearance that you are not able to change.

 If you are satisfied with the way you look, that's great! If you are not, you may often think or say things like "I'm too thin." "My hair is too curly." "I would be happy if I were taller."

When you are tempted to complain about the way you look, remember that focusing on the negative will only put you in a bad mood. Here are some better ways to deal with your feelings:

## Unscramble the letters.

**1. Don't put yourself _ _ _ _ . (ondw) Instead of complaining about the features you are not happy with, focus on things you do like about yourself and the things you are good at.**

25

**2.** Don't _ _ _ _ _ _ _ (eparcom) yourself to other girls. Comparing yourself to others may cause you to become insecure, and feel like you are never good enough. Remind yourself that every girl is valuable and unique. Be glad that we all have similarities and differences because the world would be a boring place if everyone was exactly the same.

**3.** Accept what you cannot _ _ _ _ _ _ (hancge). There is no such thing as a foot-shrinking machine for girls with large feet. The body you have is the only one that you're going to get. Try to appreciate it and take good care of it!

**4.** Make a _ _ _ _ (alnp) to change the things you can change. Here's an example: if you feel that you are over-weight or underweight, ask your parents if you can talk to your doctor. The doctor can make suggestions that will help you achieve your goal to be healthy.

**5.** Be _ _ _ _ (oury) best, and do your best. Practice good hygiene. Keep your body, your hair and your clothing clean. Exercise and eat foods that are good for you. Take good care of your mind and body. Learn all that you can in school. Choose books, movies and music that have a positive message. Have fun with friends and family. Treat others with kindness and respect, and choose friends who are kind and respectful to you.

# Gateway Pass-Word

YOUSTON TOUR PART 2

So far, the Girl Guides have helped you to focus on your point of view and the many different ideas about outward appearances. Consider what you've learned and write a message about outer beauty to inspire others.

_____

_____

_____

_____

_____

_____

# Part 💮💮
## Checking The Inside Out

# A-Mazing Personality

## Be yourself and be amazing

Wow! What a cool place.

Where are we now?

This is the center of YOUston. It's called "Amazing Personality." It's the place where a girl thinks and feels.

I think I feel lost.

Sometimes a girl's thoughts and feelings are quite simply, complex.

That doesn't make any sense.

Sure it does. Once the Girl Reader answers a few questions, her personality will be a little clearer.

This girl has got personality!
Answer these questions to find out more.

**1.** **What is your favorite season? What do you like most about it? Name an aroma that makes you think of your favorite season.**

_____

_____

_____

_____

**2.** What kind of music do you like most? Least? Write the name of your favorite artist and the name of your favorite song.

_____

_____

_____

_____

**3.** What kinds of foods do you like-junk, health, home made, ethnic (for example, Chinese or Mexican)? What's your very favorite dish?

_____

_____

_____

_____

**4.** What is your favorite color? What is your favorite flavor?

- - - - - - - - - - - - - - - - - - - - - - - - -

- - - - - - - - - - - - - - - - - - - - - - - - -

- - - - - - - - - - - - - - - - - - - - - - - - -

- - - - - - - - - - - - - - - - - - - - - - - - -

# What are you like? What do you like?

Answer based on your natural reactions—not the reactions you think others would expect. Rate the following from 1 to 5:

😃 😊 😐 🙁 😖

*1-really like*  *2-like*  *3-don't mind*  *4-dislike*  *5-really dislike*

**1.** I ⬤ **hanging out with my friends.**

**2.** I ⬤ **spending time alone.**

**3.** I ⬤ **meeting new people.**

**4.** I ⬤ **texting and spending time on social media.**

**5.** I ⬤ **taking and posting selfies.**

**6.** I ⬤ **leading a group game or project.**

So, I think ....          Mmhmmm...

**7.** I ⬤ **listening to others, even if their ideas are different from my own.**

8. I ⬤ when someone tells me I did something wrong and corrects me.

9. I ⬤ learning about people who are different from me.

10. I ⬤ trying new activities or exploring new places.

11. I ⬤ performing in front of an audience.

12. I ⬤ doing something creative like drawing, writing a story or making music.

13. I ⬤ pitching in when there is work to be done.

14. I ⬤ saying nice things about other people.

15. I ⬤ comforting a friend who is sad.

**Will you tell the truth and nothing but the truth?**
**Choose one of the words listed below to fill in the blanks.**
**Write the answers based on the way you really feel.**

never    rarely    sometimes    often    always

1. I am _____ right.
2. I _____ try to look at the bright side of things.
3. I _____ blame someone else for my mistakes.
4. I _____ complain.
5. I _____ show gratitude to others.
6. I _____ listen to or spread gossip.
7. I _____ support others with a friendly smile or encouraging words.
8. I _____ follow the rules.
9. I _____ deliberately break the rules.
10. I _____ interrupt or talk over people so I can get my point across.
11. I _____ share my things.
12. I am _____ neat and well organized.
13. I _____ lose and misplace things.
14. I _____ wait until the last minute to do my homework.

33

# Which tee shirt describes your personality?
## Choose one or design your own.

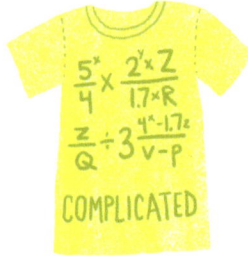

CUDDLY

CRANKY

$$\frac{5^x}{4} \times \frac{2^y \times Z}{1.7 \times R}$$
$$\frac{Z}{Q} \div 3\frac{4^x - 1.7z}{v - p}$$

COMPLICATED

You have learned that there are many different ideas about outward beauty, and those ideas may change from one culture to another. But in every culture inner beauty, what a girl is like on the inside, should be most important . Girls show their inner beauty in the way they behave and treat others.

## Circle the personality traits that reveal inner beauty.

Loving or Hateful
Kind or Cruel
Gentle or Harsh
Helpful or Hurtful
Thankful or Ungrateful
Generous or Stingy
Respectful or Disrespectful

### Which of the qualities above do your friends and family see in you?

_____

_____

_____

## List the qualities that you want to practice more.

_____

_____

_____

_____

## How will you practice the inner beauty qualities more?

_____

_____

## LIST THE QUALITIES THAT YOU WANT TO AVOID.

_____

_____

_____

_____

## How will you avoid the qualities that are not beautiful?

-------------------------------

-------------------------------

-------------------------------

-------------------------------

## Grow your good character traits

Welcome to the Inner Me Market. Hopefully you will choose personality traits that are good for you. A kind and respectful personality isn't just good and healthy for the girl who has it, but it's also helpful to the people around her. Other girls will see that she's pleasant to hang out with, and she may inspire them to be kind and respectful too.

The Inner Me Market is also a good place to learn that the outside of a package is not as important as what is on the inside—just like a girl's outward appearance is less important than what she's like on the inside (her character or personality).

**Which shopping cart will you choose?**
**Circle the one you like best.**

Circle the food items that you will
put in your shopping cart.

Circle the flowers and plants you will
take home to brighten your space.

POISON IVY

Your shopping is complete. You've made your choices.
Now it's time to purchase your items and take them
home. Choose the shopping bag that you will use.

**Use the space below to write about your choices. Which shopping cart did you choose? Why did you choose it?**

? _____
  _____
  _____
  _____

*Which food items did you choose? Why did you choose them?*

- - - - - - - - - - - - - - - - - - - - - -
- - - - - - - - - - - - - - - - - - - - - -
- - - - - - - - - - - - - - - - - - - - - -
- - - - - - - - - - - - - - - - - - - - - -
- - - - - - - - - - - - - - - - - - - - - -

? **Which plants did you decide NOT to put in your shopping basket? Why?** ?

- - - - - - - - - - - - - - - - - - - - - -
- - - - - - - - - - - - - - - - - - - - - -
- - - - - - - - - - - - - - - - - - - - - -
- - - - - - - - - - - - - - - - - - - - - -

**Describe the shopping bags you did not choose. What was the reason you didn't choose them?**

- - - - - - - - - - - - - - - - - - - - - -
- - - - - - - - - - - - - - - - - - - - - -
- - - - - - - - - - - - - - - - - - - - - -
- - - - - - - - - - - - - - - - - - - - - -

You can apply this shopping rule to a girl's inner beauty: Don't choose bad fruit and harmful plants because they are unhealthy and unpleasant even if you put them inside a pretty shopping cart or bag.

A girl's bad behavior and unkindness toward others is like bad fruit and harmful plants. Bad behavior and unkindness include bullying—in person or on social media, teasing, and deliberately leaving others out of activities and games.

### Use the space below if you can think of more bad behaviors and ways to be unkind.

_____

_____

_____

_____

If a girl is unkind and behaves badly, it doesn't really matter how she looks on the outside. What she's like on the inside can create a healthy pleasant atmosphere or unhealthy unpleasant atmosphere.

# Family Tree

## Be a tree hugger

Every family is different, and your family is a very important part of who you are. The following questions will focus on what your family is like.

1. **Which family members do you live with? Place the correct number in the spaces provided. (Example: I live with 2 sisters.)**

   ___Mom ___Dad
   ___Stepmom ___Stepdad
   ___Sister ___Brother
   ___Grandmother ___Grandfather
   ___Stepsister ___Stepbrother

2. **Which of your family members do you admire and why?**

   _____
   _____
   _____

**3.** Choose the words that best describe where you and your family live. My family and I live:

_____ in a house.

_____ on a farm or ranch.

_____ in an apartment.

_____ on a boat.

_____ in a town house.

_____ in a pineapple under the sea.

_____ none of the above. (write your own description below)

_____

**4.** My family and I live: (mark an X for all that apply)

_____ in a big city.

_____ in a small town.

_____ in a quiet neighborhood.

_____ on a busy street.

_____ in a warm climate where it
       doesn't get very cold in the winter.

_____ in a cold climate where it's really
       cold and snowy in the winter.

**5.** If you could live anywhere in the world, where would it
be and why? _____

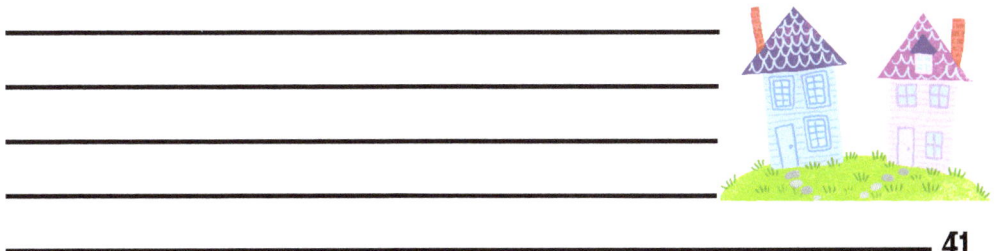

_____

_____

_____

_____

Have you ever heard someone say, "The apple doesn't fall far from the tree?" It means that a son or daughter is a lot like their mom or dad. Even if you are adopted and you don't physically look like your parents, you can still grow to be like them in other ways. Maybe you take on some of their habits like biting your lip when you're nervous. Or you may take on some of their personality traits (being friendly and helpful) or their interests (a love for sports or music.)

**Which physical or personality traits did you get from your mom or dad? Write your answers on the apples.**

**1.** Does your family enjoy any traditions or customs? If so, what are they? It can be something as simple as watching a movie together every Friday night.

_____

_____

_____

_____

_____

_____

_____

_____

_____

_____

_____

_____

**2.** Do you look forward to joining in on the traditions and customs? Why or why not?

_____

_____

_____

_____

_____

**3. Does your family practice a religion or certain beliefs? If so, what is the name of your religion and what important things have you learned from it?**

_____

_____

_____

_____

_____

_____

**4. Does your religion or beliefs include regular gatherings at a place of worship? If so, how often do you attend these gatherings? What happens while you are there?**

_____

_____

_____

_____

**5. Write about one of the most fun outings or events you shared with your family.**

- - - - - - - - - - - - - - - - - - - - - - -

- - - - - - - - - - - - - - - - - - - - - - -

- - - - - - - - - - - - - - - - - - - - - - -

# Friend Observatory

## Good friend – find one, be one

It's great to have good friends and to be a good friend. Answer the questions below to take a closer look at your friendships.

### 1. Write the names of two of your closest friends.

_____

_____

## 2. Write one thing that you really like about ♥ each of the two friends. ♥

---------------------------------

---------------------------------

---------------------------------

### 3.What activities do you enjoy with your friends?

------------------------------------

------------------------------------

------------------------------------

------------------------------------

------------------------------------

### 4.Write about a time when one of your friends did something that made you feel happy.

_____

_____

_____

_____

_____

## 5. Write about a time when you did something that made your friend feel happy.

_____

_____

_____

_____

Underline the sentences that describe things a good friend would do.

- She would share her lunch with me if I forgot to bring mine.

- She would tease me and call me names that hurt my feelings.

- She would leave me out of the group when her other friends are around.

- She would surprise me by decorating my locker on my birthday.

- She would stick up for me if she heard someone saying bad things behind my back.

- She would treat me with kindness and respect.

# Fun Center

## Have a little or a lot

This looks like a fun place to be.

There are so many things to do here.

Welcome to the YOUston FunCenter.

## What kind of activities do you like?

Mark the W if you like to watch the sport or activity. Mark the P if you participate or would like to participate in the sport or activity. Mark both the W and P if you like to watch and participate. Mark the N if you're not interested.

## Sports

Volleyball  W  P  N
Basketball  W  P  N
Football  W  P  N
Baseball  W  P  N
Swimming  W  P  N
Horseback Riding  W  P  N
Tennis  W  P  N

In the space below, add any sports activity that you enjoy that was not listed. _____

_____

_____

# Music

Marching Band   W P N

Orchestra   W P N

Pop Band   W P N

Jazz Band   W P N

Choir   W P N

In the space below, list the instruments that you play or would like to learn to play. _____

_____

_____

# Dance

Ballet  W P N

Modern  W P N

Folk  W P N

Hip Hop  W P N

Cheer/Dance Team  W P N

Tap  W P N

Line  W P N

In the space below, add any dance activity that you enjoy that was not listed. _____

_____

_____

# Entertainment

Live Theatre  W  P  N

Movies  W  P  N

Video Games  W  P  N

Amusement Parks  W  P  N

Museums  W  P  N

In the space below, list the types of entertainment that you are interested in that were not listed. _____

_____

_____

# Hobbies

Sewing  W  P  N

Arts and Crafts  W  P  N

Painting/Sketching  W  P  N

Photography  W  P  N

Writing  W  P  N

In the space below, list the hobbies that you are interested in that were not listed. _____

_____

_____

**1.** **What is the name of your school? Is it a public, private or home school?**

_____

_____

_____

_____

**2. What do you like about school?**

-----------------------------------------

-----------------------------------------

-----------------------------------------

-----------------------------------------

-----------------------------------------

-----------------------------------------

**3. What are your favorite subjects?**

-----------------------------------------

-----------------------------------------

-----------------------------------------

-----------------------------------------

**4. Which subjects do you do well in?**

_____

_____

_____

_____

_____

_____

**5. Which subjects would you like to improve in?**

**6. Do you think that it is important to learn and do well in school? Why or why not?**

_____

_____

_____

_____

Have you ever heard anyone say, "Knowledge is power?" What do you think it means? The saying, "Knowledge is power" is similar to the saying, "Give a girl a fish and you feed her for a day. Teach her to fish, and she can feed herself for a lifetime." In other words, it's important for a girl to learn new things that will help her to become more independent.

**List two things that you learned at school or at home that have helped you to become more independent. (Here's an example: Have you learned new vocabulary words in school that help you communicate better?)**

_____

_____

_____

**If you could create the perfect school, what would it be like? What kind of teachers would be there and what subjects would they teach?**

-------------------------------

-------------------------------

-------------------------------

-------------------------------

-------------------------------

*What kind of job or career would you like to have when you grow up?*

-------------------------------

-------------------------------

# End of Tour Pass-Word

## Time to say good-bye

**Congratulations!** You have completed the tour of the ever-growing, ever-changing "YOUston." Hopefully, you learned new things, had a good time, and decided to become an iGrow Girl!

You should continue your adventure by discovering new things about yourself, as well as the people and the world around you each day. Try to be honest about who you are, and look for the beauty in you and in other girls. Make an effort to develop positive ideas and habits that will help you grow, improve, and inspire others. Make good choices for your physical and mental health. Do your best in your studies, and be kind and fair in your relationships. Pay attention to your words and habits. When they are not positive, stop and choose to think and behave in a better way.

We hope you had fun on your tour of YOUston!

And we hope you will become an iGrow Girl, too.

I grow. You grow. We grow together!

END OF YOUSTON TOUR

Make a plan to keep your work book in a safe place so that you can return to it and review your answers from time to time. You might be surprised to see how your appearance and preferences transform as you get older.

In the space below, write a note to your future self about the things you've learned on the tour and how you hope to grow.

The certificate below states that you have successfully completed this tour. Remember that the trip through YOUston will continue as long as you grow and change. Never stop growing and exploring the unique person that you are.

# Certificate of Completion

This certifies that

_____

YOUR NAME

has successfully completed a tour of YOUston

_____

TODAY'S DATE

This girl has a pretty good idea of who she is!

Check the box below if you want
to be an iGrowGirl

❑ YES! I am an iGrowGirl.

I will continue to discover the real me and be
true to myself.  I will develop positive ideas and habits
that will help me grow, improve, and inspire others.
I will learn new things and make good choices
for my physical and mental health.  I will do my best in
my studies and be kind and fair in my relationships.

I will learn about words and habits that are not positive.
When those words describe my behavior, I will stop
and choose to think and behave in a better way.

_____

SIGNATURE OF WITNESS
(Mom or someone else who took the tour with you)